# Finding Aunt Maria

**Adrienne Frater**
Illustrated by Denise Durkin

WORLD
ATLAS

# Contents

Chapter 1

# Goodbye, Aunt Maria

It took forever to get to the airport. As they pulled into the parking lot, Linda's sigh filled the car. When no one asked what was bothering her, she sighed again.

"Okay," said Dad. "We know you don't want Aunt Maria to leave, but it's her job. You're lucky to have an aunt who's a movie director and travels all over the world."

When she wasn't away directing movies, Aunt Maria lived with Linda and her family. She was Linda's favorite person.

"Cheer up," said Aunt Maria, as they unloaded the trunk. "I'll send postcards." Linda gave a wobbly grin. When her aunt was directing a movie in Thailand, her walls were covered with postcards of elephants

and tropical forests. When her aunt directed a movie in Egypt, her walls were covered with postcards of camels and pyramids.

"You said this movie's being filmed in the United States," said Linda.

"Uh-huh. But it's an **exotic** location, a long way from here."

Linda wheeled one of her aunt's bags to the check-in counter. She tried to be cheerful, but her grin kept slipping.

"I'll e-mail you when I get there," said Aunt Maria.

"Get *where*?" asked Linda.

A cunning look slid onto Aunt Maria's face. "What if I don't tell you? What if I put clues into each e-mail? We can play *Where in the World Is Aunt Maria?*"

For the first time that day Linda laughed. There was nothing she and Aunt Maria liked better than playing games.

All the way home in the car, Linda thought about exotic places a long way from home.

---

**exotic** – unusual or different

Chapter 2

# The Search Begins!

Linda couldn't wait for her aunt's first e-mail. The next day she checked the computer again and again. She was scowling at the *no new messages* icon, when her brother Carlos walked past. He was carrying his precious basketball.

"Hi," Linda said.

Carlos grunted. He wasn't very interested in talking to his little sister now that he'd turned thirteen. Then a new message popped up.

Hi,
What a LONG flight! There were two flights, in fact. On the first, I sat next to twins glued to computer games. On the second, I sat next to a Japanese-American couple traveling to visit their new grandchild. When the plane landed, we were welcomed with music and the night air smelled sweet.
Love,
Aunt M.

Linda printed the e-mail and highlighted *LONG flight,* and *music* and *the night air smelled sweet.*

"What are you doing?" asked Carlos.

"Homework," Linda said. She wanted to keep the game between herself and Aunt Maria. And she wanted to solve the mystery on her own!

***

That night, Linda thought about far-away places that smelled sweet. She thought about deserts, mountains, and wide blue lakes. As she fell asleep, she imagined that she could hear distant music.

## Chapter 3

# Curious Carlos

The next day, Linda couldn't wait for school to end.

"Suzi," she asked her friend as they left school, "where would you go for a vacation if you could choose *any* place in the United States?"

"Florida," said Suzi. She zipped up her jacket and caught a snowflake on her tongue.

When Linda got home, she raced upstairs and turned the computer on. There was an e-mail from Aunt Maria.

> Hi,
> Although everyone here speaks English, I could say *Hi* in many languages. Today I was in meetings all day. Tomorrow we start filming, so we are leaving the city to head for the mountains and ocean. What? No more clues? If I make it TOO easy, it will take away the fun.
> Love,
> Aunt M.

"She *can't* be in Florida," thought Linda. "There are no mountains there." She printed the e-mail and slipped it into her pocket. She didn't want Carlos to see it.

"What's up?" asked Carlos, walking into the room. "I've never seen you so interested in the computer before."

"Nothing," said Linda. She looked across the hall into her brother's messy room. There was a brand new atlas on his bed! Linda's eyes grew as round as frisbees.

"Hey, where did you get that atlas?" she asked.

"You tell me what you're up to on the computer and I'll tell you," Carlos replied.

"I'm trying to find Aunt Maria," Linda said as she laid the e-mails on the desk. "She's sending me clues about where she's working in the United States. It's kind of like a game."

Carlos crossed the hall and picked up the atlas from his bed. "I ordered this atlas online. You can use it if you like."

Linda was surprised that Carlos had bought an atlas. She knew he had been saving his allowance for something, but she thought it would be a new basketball, not an atlas! She grinned. Maybe her brother was just as curious about the world as she was.

"Hmm." Carlos read the e-mails, and then opened the atlas to a map of the United States. Each state was a different color, and they fit together like a jigsaw puzzle.

"I need a map that shows landforms like mountains, valleys, and lakes," said Linda.

Their heads were still bent over the atlas when Mom called them for supper.

***

As she ate her meatballs, Linda couldn't stop thinking about Aunt Maria. Where could she be?

"Remember, she took two flights," she said to Carlos, waving her fork. "I think she's on the **West Coast**."

"Yes," said Carlos, slurping spaghetti. "Somewhere with mountains *and* ocean."

**West Coast** – the part of the United States that is along the Pacific Ocean

Chapter 4

# More Clues

The next day, school seemed to last forever. Linda was fidgety all day. The night before, she and Carlos had used the atlas and walked their fingers along all the mountains on the West Coast.

"Remember, Aunt Maria spent her first two days in the city," Carlos had said.

"Maybe she was in Seattle, San Francisco, or Los Angeles," Linda had replied.

As soon as school was over, Linda raced home. Carlos tossed his basketball impatiently while they waited for the computer to boot. "Yes!" said Linda as a new e-mail popped up.

Hi,
I just went for an awesome walk and discovered trees and birds I've never seen before. It's so relaxing knowing there are no snakes or poison ivy here. After filming today, I enjoyed some shaved ice. Enough clues. I'm giving too much away.
Love,
Aunt M.

After searching the Internet, Linda and Carlos deleted all the places with snakes and poison ivy.

***

That night, Linda thought about ice. Was Aunt Maria in a country with icebergs, glaciers, and snow? By the time she fell asleep, thoughts of cold places had given her goose bumps.

Chapter 5

# The Forgotten States

The next day there was no e-mail. The next two days were disappointing, too. On the fourth day, Linda jiggled her foot as she waited, expecting the icon to say *no new messages* again, but she was wrong! On the screen was another e-mail and more clues.

> Hi,
> Sorry for the silence. I've been up in the mountains. They looked close on the map, but the road twisted and turned like a snake. It was so windy up there that the waterfalls flowed upside-down. (It's true!) From the top of the mountain I saw humpback whales! Tonight I learned that the indigenous people here tell their stories through dance. Tomorrow we're filming from boats out on the ocean.
> Love,
> Aunt M.

"What's does *indigenous* mean?" asked Linda.

Carlos was already thumbing through the dictionary. "It means *native*, not visitors," he said.

Linda frowned at the map. "Mountains, birds, trees . . . " she muttered.

"And no snakes," Carlos added.

Linda flipped through the atlas. "We've forgotten something!" she shrieked.

"What's that?"

"We've forgotten the other two states!"

***

Linda and Carlos argued all the way through supper.

"She must be in Alaska," said Carlos. "It's full of mountains."

"There are mountains in Hawaii, too," said Linda. "And strange birds and trees and lots of different languages. I think Aunt Maria's in Hawaii."

"But what about the humpback whales and shaved ice?" asked Carlos. "I think she's in Alaska."

Chapter 6

# The Mystery Solved!

As they opened the fifth e-mail, Carlos breathed down his sister's neck.

> Hi,
> We had trouble filming today. There were too many boards. But at least when it's too windy in one spot, you can move to another. I was STARVING by lunch and ate two plates of poi and a bowl of macadamia nuts. Tomorrow we fly to a new location where there's lava and steam. E-mail me when you've figured out where I am!
> Love,
> Aunt M.

There was silence while Carlos and Linda surfed the Internet. First they looked up volcanoes, then macadamia nuts and poi.

"Yes!" yelled Linda, reading from the computer screen. "It says here that poi is a sweet dish made from taro root. And taro grows in tropical places. It's GOT to be Hawaii!"

"But the *boards* could be snowboards, not surfboards," muttered Carlos, who was now searching on the Internet for humpback whales. "And don't forget that Alaska has volcanoes, too."

"But Aunt Maria said, *'when it's too windy in one spot, you can move to another.'* That means she's on an island."

"Why?"

"Your atlas says that when it's windy on one side of an island, it can be calm on the other. The only things that don't make sense are the whales."

"They DO make sense!" yelled Carlos suddenly, pointing at the computer. "It says here, *'Humpback whales spend the winter in Hawaiian waters.'* I think we've found Aunt Maria!"

Linda and Carlos e-mailed their aunt right away. Later that night, she replied.

Hi,
Yes, I'm in Hawaii! One of these days you might be lucky enough to visit here, too!
See you soon,
Aunt M.

P.S.
I've attached a digital photo that somebody took of me!

A week later, a large package arrived. Carlos helped Linda rip it open. "Look!" said Linda. She unwrapped a box of chocolate-covered macadamia nuts, a ukulele, and a hula skirt.

Linda read the note from Aunt Maria. It said, *'Well done! Here's the prize for finding me.'*

"You can play the ukulele while I dance," Linda said to Carlos as she tried on the hula skirt.

But Carlos didn't answer. He and the macadamia nuts had disappeared.

DAMIA

# The Facts Behind the Story

## Alaska and Hawaii

There are 50 states in the United States of America. 48 of the states are together. Alaska and Hawaii are the only two states that are separate. They were also the last two states to join the United States, in 1959.

This map shows where Alaska and Hawaii are located.

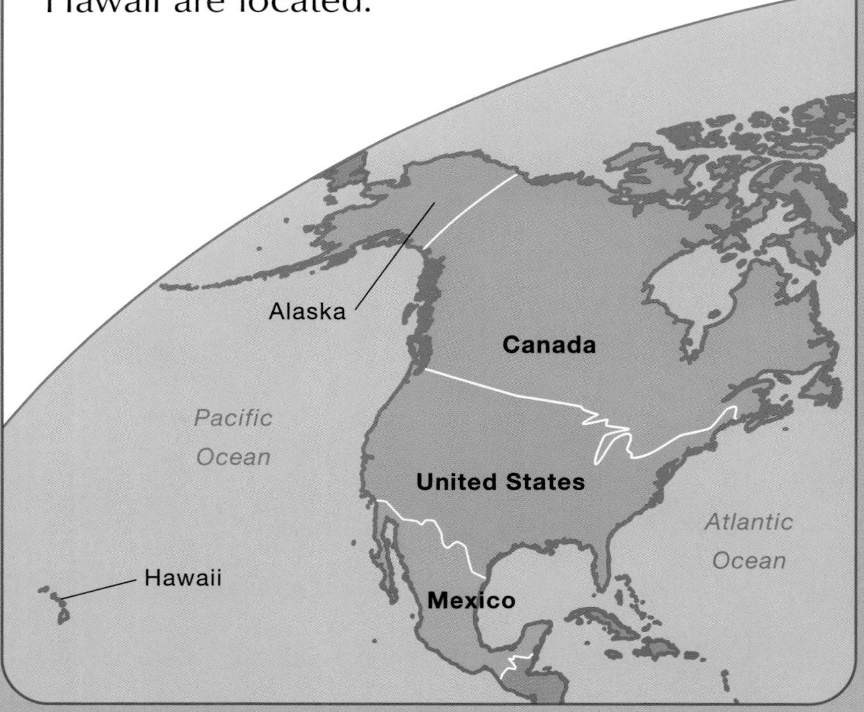

## Alaska

Alaska is farther north than any other state. It is northwest of Canada. It is the biggest state. It is more than twice the size of Texas. Alaska is also the coldest state.

## Hawaii

Hawaii is farther south than any other state. It is a group of more than 100 islands. There are eight main islands. Hawaii is one of the warmest states.

## Extend Your Reading

### Think About the Story

In *Finding Aunt Maria,* Linda and Carlos play a game with their aunt. They use e-mail clues to figure out where she has gone on a trip. Think about these questions.

- What is the first clue that Aunt Maria gives Linda? What does it mean?
- How does Linda know that Carlos is curious about geography?
- Which clue do you think is the most important? Why?

To learn more about interesting places in the world, read the books below.

**SUGGESTED READING**
**Windows on Literacy**
*Down the Nile*
*Grand Canyon Adventure*

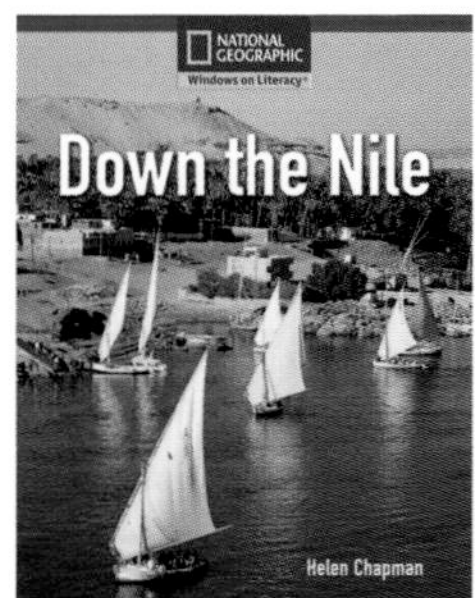


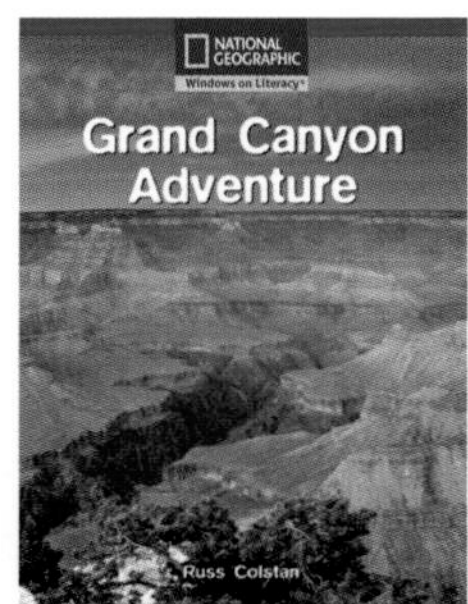